I dedicate this book to love

Chapter 1: A World of Uncharted Emotion

In the vast expanse of the human experience, our emotional landscapes are like uncharted territories, brimming with an endless array of sentiments. Just as explorers embark on journeys into unfamiliar lands, we traverse through the depths of our own hearts, navigating the intricacies of our emotions.

Emotions shape our perception of the world, giving it depth and meaning beyond what meets the eye. They are the threads that weave through the fabric of our existence, influencing our thoughts, actions, and interactions with others. At times, they can be uplifting and exhilarating, lifting our spirits to new heights. Other times, they can be overwhelming and heavy, dragging us into the depths of despair. Nonetheless, emotions are an integral part of our human nature, guiding us through the rollercoaster of life.

Imagine a vibrant tapestry, each thread depicting a different emotion. The colors are vibrant, ranging from the fiery red of passion to the serene blue of tranquility. Every moment adds a new stitch, blending shades to create a kaleidoscope of feelings. Joy, sorrow, excitement, fear, love, and anger are just a few of the countless hues that color this tapestry.

As we journey through the chapters of our lives, our emotions serve as both the navigational compass and the compass' needle. They guide our choices and decisions, influencing the paths we choose to take. Like whispers in our ears, they offer guidance, urging us towards what brings us joy and warning us of potential hardships. While reason may provide a map, it is emotion that breathes life into our decisions, infusing them with passion and conviction.

Our emotions also play a profound role in shaping our connections to others. They create the invisible threads that bind us in shared experiences, establishing bonds of empathy and understanding. When we share a laugh, it's because joy has connected us. When we mourn alongside a friend, it's because sorrow has united us. Through our emotions, we not only navigate the ever-changing landscape within ourselves but also forge connections with the hearts of those we encounter.

In this book, we invite you on an extraordinary journey through the workings of the heart. Together, we will delve into the depths of our emotional world, exploring the vastness of this uncharted territory. Through stories, reflections, and insights, we will unravel the complexities of our emotions, peering into the matter that gives life meaning and color.

Whether you find yourself standing atop the highest peaks of joy or trudging through the darkest valleys of despair, remember that your emotions are a testament to your humanity. They are the brushstrokes that paint the canvas of your life, creating a masterpiece uniquely your own. So, let us embark on this adventure together, in search of understanding and connection in a world overflowing with uncharted emotion.

Chapter 2: The Origins and Complexities of Emotion

To comprehend the labyrinthine realm of emotions, we must first unravel their origins and complexities. Emotions have played a crucial role in the survival and evolution of our species, shaping our behavior and enabling us to navigate the world effectively. By tracing their roots back to our ancestors, we can begin to understand why emotions are such a fundamental aspect of our human experience.

In the annals of our evolutionary history, emotions served as a survival mechanism, helping our prehistoric ancestors adapt and respond to their environment. The fight-or-flight response, for example, was essential for our early ancestors when faced with dangerous predators or precarious situations. Their emotions enabled them to react swiftly, either by confronting the threat head-on or seeking safety in retreat. This primal instinct still persists within us today, acting as a subconscious guide to our responses in threatening situations.

As we transition from the evolutionary origins of emotions to their neuroscientific underpinnings, we begin to unravel the complex web that connects our brains, hormones, and neural pathways. Our emotions are not merely mind-based experiences but are heavily influenced by the intricate workings of our physiological systems. In recent years, neuroscientists have made remarkable strides in deciphering the neural correlates of emotions.

Within our brains, a myriad of regions collaboratively orchestrate the experience and expression of emotions. The amygdala, a small almond-shaped structure deep within the brain, is particularly involved in the processing and generation of emotional responses. It scans our surroundings, assessing potential threats or rewards, and determines the appropriate emotional reactions to be elicited.

These signals are then relayed to other regions, such as the prefrontal cortex, which plays a crucial role in regulating and modulating our emotional experiences.

However, emotions are not solely the result of our brain's activity but are also influenced by a complex interplay of hormones coursing through our bodies. Hormones, such as cortisol and adrenaline, are released in response to emotional stimuli, heightening our awareness, and preparing us for action. The delicate balance between neurotransmitters and hormones helps to shape and color our emotional experiences, lending to their intensity or subtlety.

Nevertheless, emotions are exquisitely complex, and a reductionist understanding of their origins and mechanisms falls short of capturing their true essence. To devise a comprehensive understanding, we must also consider the psychological and social dimensions at play. Our emotions are shaped by our unique cognitive and perceptual processes, which interpret the world and assign meaning to our experiences. Cultural, social, and individual factors further contribute to the tapestry of our emotional landscape, influencing the range of emotions we experience and how we express them.

By weaving together the threads of biology and psychology, we begin to gain insight into the complexities of emotions. However, this is an ongoing journey of exploration, as new research and discoveries continuously contribute to our understanding. The study of emotions is a multidisciplinary endeavor, encompassing fields such as psychology, neuroscience, anthropology, and sociology. Only by embracing these diverse perspectives can we carve a path through the intricate maze of emotions and truly comprehend the rich tapestry of our emotional lives.

In the following chapters, we will delve deeper into the specific emotions that color our existence, exploring their distinct qualities, functions, and manifestations. From joy to sadness, fear to love, each emotion carries its own unique fingerprint, and by unraveling their complexities, we can gain a deeper appreciation for the kaleidoscope of human experience.

Chapter 3: The Spectrum of Joy and Its Sublime Variations

Among the myriad of emotions, joy stands as a radiant beacon, illuminating our lives with its brilliance. In this chapter, we embark on a quest to understand the vast spectrum of joy and its sublime variations. From the simple pleasures that light up our everyday lives to the profound euphoria of achieving long-held aspirations, we explore how joy manifests itself and reverberates through our being. Through captivating anecdotes and scientific revelations, we delve into the profound impact of joy on our overall well-being and personal growth.

Imagine waking up to the gentle caress of sunlight pouring through the curtains, as birds outside sing their melodic symphony; this, too, is part of the spectrum of joy. It is found in the small moments that we often overlook – a warm cup of coffee on a chilly morning or the soft purr of a contented cat curled up beside us. These simple pleasures remind us of the beauty inherent in life's everyday occurrences.

As we move through the spectrum, we encounter moments where joy takes a grander form. Imagine the exultation of a painter who steps back to admire a masterpiece; the thrill of a musician playing their composition in front of a captivated audience; or the elation of an athlete crossing the finish line, breaking personal records. These deeper moments of joy are born out of dedication, hard work, and the pursuit of one's passions. They embody the satisfaction of progress and achievement, fueling our desires to further explore our potential.

Joy does not merely exist in the realm of personal accomplishments, but also thrives in our connections with others. Picture the joy that lingers in the air during a family gathering, where laughter and love intertwine, leaving us with a warm feeling in our hearts. This pure, unadulterated joy is channeled through the bonds we share with our loved ones, reminding us of the importance of cultivating meaningful relationships.

Alongside these personal experiences of joy, scientific discoveries reveal the powerful impact it has on our well-being and personal growth. Studies have shown that joyful moments release endorphins, dopamine, and serotonin – chemicals that enhance our mood and reduce stress. Harnessing the power of joy in our lives can lead to improved mental and physical health, increased resilience, and a greater sense of purpose. By understanding and consciously seeking out joy, we empower ourselves to navigate life's challenges with resilience and hope.

The spectrum of joy is not static nor one-dimensional. It meanders and shifts, encompassing experiences that range from a whisper to a roar, from a light flicker to a blazing fire, from a contented sigh to an exuberant shout. It is a kaleidoscope of emotions, each unique in its composition and intensity. To open ourselves up to the full spectrum of joy, we must embrace its many shades and nuances, recognizing that joy, in all its forms, is an inherent part of our humanity.

Joy is a complex and multifaceted emotion that can be experienced in various hues, each intertwined with different aspects of our lives. When we immerse ourselves in exploring these hues, we begin to understand that joy goes beyond mere happiness and pleasure. It becomes a state of being that is intricately linked to gratitude, mindfulness, and resilience.

Gratitude is the first hue of joy, as it brings an awareness and appreciation for the blessings and positive experiences in our lives. When we practice gratitude, we actively acknowledge and give thanks for the small and big things that bring joy into our days. Whether it's the warmth of a smile, the beauty of nature, or the love of family and friends, gratitude amplifies our joyful experiences.

Mindfulness, the second hue of joy, is the practice of being fully present and engaged in the present moment, without judgment. When we approach life with mindful awareness, we open ourselves up to experiencing joy in even the simplest of moments. Whether it's savoring the taste of a delicious meal, feeling the warmth of the sun on our skin, or relishing in a moment of connection with someone, mindfulness allows us to fully immerse ourselves in these joyful experiences.

Resilience is the third hue of joy, as it enables us to navigate through life's challenges and setbacks with grace and a positive outlook. When we cultivate resilience, we develop the ability to bounce back from difficult situations and find joy amidst adversity. It's the capacity to find strength and meaning in the face of hardships, knowing that joy can be found on the other side of struggle.

True joy is not an isolated experience but rather intricately woven into the fabric of our lives. It emerges when we cultivate gratitude, practice mindfulness, and develop resilience. By consciously exploring and embracing these different hues of joy, we can deepen our appreciation for the moments that bring brightness into our lives.

When we become aware of the diverse facets of joy, we also realize that joy is not solely dependent on external circumstances. It can be found in the simplest of moments, in the beauty of nature, in acts of kindness, or in the stillness of our own hearts. Joy becomes a way of being, a lens through which we see and experience the world.

With this understanding, we can cultivate a deeper appreciation for the moments that ignite joy within us. We can consciously seek out joy in our daily lives, becoming attuned to the small things that bring a sense of fulfillment and connectedness. By embracing the multifaceted nature of joy, we open ourselves up to personal growth and a richer, more fulfilling existence.

Chapter 4: The Bittersweet Symphony of Sadness Sadness

Delving into the essence of sadness requires an exploration of its many faces and the underlying reasons behind its manifestation in the human experience. To truly understand sadness, it is essential to delve into its philosophical underpinnings and contemplate the profound perspectives of influential thinkers throughout history.

Friedrich Nietzsche, a renowned philosopher, questioned the value of sadness in human existence. He believed that sadness, along with pain and suffering, played a crucial role in strengthening and refining individuals. Nietzsche argued that these challenging emotions were necessary for personal growth and the development of a resilient and authentic self. Through his writings, Nietzsche challenges us to reconsider our perception of sadness as a negative force and instead view it as a catalyst for transformation.

Albert Camus, another philosophical luminary, explored the existential meaning of sadness in his works. He contended that sadness was an inevitable consequence of the human condition, a result of the innate tension between our desire for meaning and the inherent absurdity of existence. For Camus, embracing sadness was an acknowledgement of the inherent struggle and an affirmation of the richness of human experience. By facing the void and finding meaning within it, even in the midst of sadness, Camus suggests that we can find a profound sense of purpose.

Contemplating the philosophical underpinnings of sadness raises important questions about its nature and purpose. Is sadness an inherent part of life, inseparable from the human experience? Can it be a catalyst for personal growth and self-discovery, pushing individuals to confront their innermost fears and desires? Moreover, how does sadness shape our understanding of joy and happiness, casting light upon the intricacies of the human soul?

By embracing sadness as an integral part of the human experience, we gain a deeper appreciation for the delicate and intricate dance between light and dark within ourselves. Sadness allows us to understand the depths of joy, enabling us to fully appreciate the nuances of happiness. It becomes a prism through which we can explore our own emotional landscapes and navigate the complexities of the human condition.

Ultimately, by delving into the essence of sadness and considering its philosophical underpinnings, we gain a greater understanding of our own emotions and the profound impact they have on our lives. It encourages us to embrace sadness as an opportunity for growth and self-discovery, fostering a deeper appreciation for the intricate tapestry of human existence.

Navigating the complexities of sadness can feel daunting and overwhelming. It can consume our thoughts, leaving us feeling disoriented and lost, as if we are trapped in an impenetrable maze. However, there are practical strategies and techniques that can help us find our way through this emotional labyrinth.

Research from the field of psychology emphasizes the importance of self-care when facing sadness. Taking care of ourselves physically, emotionally, and mentally is crucial for navigating through difficult times. This may involve engaging in activities that bring us joy and provide us with a sense of comfort and relaxation. Engaging in hobbies, practicing self-compassion, and prioritizing rest and relaxation can all contribute to a healthier mindset and a better ability to navigate the challenges of sadness.

Seeking support from loved ones can also play a critical role in navigating sadness. Talking to someone we trust and sharing our feelings can provide much-needed comfort and validation. Loved ones can offer a listening ear and a different perspective, reminding us that we are not alone in our struggles. Their support can help us regain a sense of direction and provide us with the strength and encouragement we need to navigate the maze of sadness.

Finding healthy outlets for emotional expression is another important aspect of navigating sadness. Bottling up our emotions can intensify feelings of sadness and make it even more challenging to find our way out. Engaging in activities such as journaling, drawing, or engaging in physical exercise can help release pent-up emotions and provide a sense of relief. These outlets allow us to express ourselves authentically and explore our emotions in a safe and constructive manner.

Mindfulness techniques and coping mechanisms can also be powerful tools in navigating sadness. Mindfulness involves being fully present in the moment and accepting our emotions without judgment. By cultivating awareness and practicing mindfulness, we can observe our sadness and acknowledge it without being overwhelmed by it. Coping mechanisms such as deep breathing exercises, meditation, and grounding techniques can help us regulate our emotions and create a sense of calmness amidst the chaos.

By exploring these strategies, readers can be empowered to confront their sadness head-on and find solace in the midst of turmoil. The journey through the maze of sadness may not be easy, but with self-care, support from loved ones, healthy emotional outlets, and mindfulness techniques, it becomes possible to navigate through the complexities and eventually find a sense of peace and healing.

While sadness is often regarded as a somber and difficult emotion to process, it is important to recognize the unique beauty it holds within its depths. In moments of profound sadness, artists have found solace and inspiration, resulting in deeply poignant and moving works of art.

Literature, for instance, offers a profound avenue for exploring the complexities of sadness. Through words, authors paint vivid portraits of characters experiencing heartbreak, loss, and melancholy. From classic novels like Leo Tolstoy's "Anna Karenina," where the despair of forbidden love is palpable, to contemporary works like Markus Zusak's "The Book Thief," which delves into the tragedy of war, literature invites us to empathize with and understand the depths of human sorrow. In these narratives, we find solace in the shared experience of sadness, knowing that others have traveled the same emotional terrain.

Music, too, weaves its own melancholic tapestry, capturing the essence of sadness in its melodies and lyrics. Songs have the ability to be therapeutic, offering a cathartic release for the listener. Artists such as Adele, Billie Holiday, and Radiohead have become renowned for their ability to convey the complexity of sadness through their haunting and evocative songs. The haunting melodies, raw emotions, and poignant lyrics create a bittersweet symphony that echoes the depths of our own sadness, allowing us to find comfort and connection in the shared experience.

Visual art also plays a significant role in celebrating the unique beauty of sadness. The canvas becomes a space for artists to express their inner turmoil, transforming sorrow into visual poetry. Pieces like Vincent van Gogh's "Starry Night" and Edvard Munch's "The Scream" depict the depths of human suffering, capturing the anguish and desolation that often accompany sadness. Through these works, we find solace in knowing that even the darkest emotions can be transformed into something beautiful and meaningful.

By immersing ourselves in the art and creativity that arise from periods of profound sadness, we can discover healing and connection. The shared experience of sadness becomes a unifying force, reminding us that we are not alone in our pain. In recognizing the beauty that sadness can give rise to, we allow ourselves to appreciate the depth of our own emotions and the transformative power of art.

In concluding this chapter, we contemplate the voyage undertaken in exploring the intricate aspects of sadness. We impart a message of optimism and strength to readers, reminding them that within the orchestra of sorrow, there exists the promise of progress, recovery, and rejuvenation. By accepting the intricacies of sadness and uncovering moments of beauty amidst the darkness, we can chart a course towards enhanced comprehension and personal revelation.

Chapter 5: Navigating the Torrents of Anger and Disappointment

Section 1: The Genesis of Anger and Disappointment

Anger and disappointment often arise from unmet expectations and desires. When things don't go as planned or when we feel betrayed or let down by someone or something, these emotions can surge within us like a brewing storm. They create a sense of injustice and can ignite a fire of resentment and frustration. However, it is important to recognize that anger and disappointment are natural and valid emotions that can provide us with valuable insights into our own needs and values.

Through self-reflection, we can begin to understand the root causes of our anger and disappointment. Are our expectations realistic and reasonable? Are we projecting our own insecurities onto others? Examining our own beliefs and values can help us determine whether our emotional reaction is proportionate to the situation at hand. By gaining clarity on the origins of these emotions, we empower ourselves to respond more effectively and constructively.

Furthermore, exploring the wisdom of philosophers can offer guidance on how to navigate through anger and disappointment. Stoic philosophers like Epictetus and Marcus Aurelius remind us that we have the power to control our emotions and reactions. They encourage us to focus on what is within our control, such as our thoughts, intentions, and actions, rather than dwelling on external circumstances that are beyond our influence. By shifting our perspective and focusing on our own inner development, we can find a sense of peace amidst the storms of anger and disappointment.

Therapeutic interventions can also provide valuable tools for managing anger and disappointment. Cognitive-behavioral therapy, for example, helps individuals identify and challenge negative thought patterns and replace them with more adaptive and constructive thinking. Through therapy, individuals can develop coping strategies, such as relaxation techniques or assertiveness skills, to manage their emotions and communicate their needs effectively. By seeking professional help, individuals are guided through a process of healing and self-discovery, enabling them to transform destructive anger and disappointment into growth and personal development.

Personal anecdotes can serve as powerful sources of inspiration and guidance on the journey of understanding and managing anger and disappointment. Hearing stories from others who have faced similar struggles can offer solace and remind us that we are not alone in our experiences. Through sharing their own triumphs and struggles, individuals can inspire hope and provide practical advice on how to navigate through the turbulent waters of these emotions.

Anger and disappointment are intense emotions that can consume us if left unchecked. However, through self-reflection, philosophical wisdom, therapeutic interventions, and personal anecdotes, we can learn to harness the potent energy of these emotions constructively. By understanding the origins of our anger and disappointment, we can respond more effectively. By incorporating the wisdom of philosophers and seeking therapeutic interventions, we can navigate through these emotions with greater resilience and grace. And by seeking solace and inspiration from personal anecdotes, we can find meaning and growth in the aftermath of these turbulent storms.

Understanding the root causes of anger and disappointment requires delving into the origins of these emotions and examining the various factors that contribute to their development. In many cases, anger and disappointment can be traced back to unmet expectations, betrayal, or a sense of injustice.

Unmet expectations play a significant role in triggering anger and disappointment. When individuals have certain hopes or desires that are not fulfilled, it can lead to feelings of frustration, resentment, and ultimately anger. For example, when someone expects a promotion at work but does not receive it, they may become angry and disappointed due to the unfulfilled expectation.

Betrayal is another common source of anger and disappointment. When someone we trust or rely on betrays us, such as a friend breaking a confidence or a partner cheating, it can lead to deep feelings of anger and disappointment. Betrayal can shatter our trust in others and disrupt our sense of security, often resulting in intense emotional responses.

A sense of injustice can also fuel anger and disappointment. Witnessing or experiencing unfairness, discrimination, or inequality can trigger strong emotional reactions. When individuals perceive that they or others have been treated unfairly or unjustly, it can evoke feelings of anger and disappointment towards the individuals or systems responsible for the perceived injustice.

To gain a deeper understanding of the complex nature of anger and disappointment, it is essential to consider the impact of personal history, societal influences, and environmental factors. Personal history, including past experiences and traumas, greatly shapes how individuals respond to situations that trigger these emotions. For example, someone with a history of past betrayals may be more prone to anger or disappointment when faced with similar situations.

Societal influences also play a significant role in shaping our emotional responses. Cultural norms, expectations, and values can shape how individuals express or suppress anger and disappointment. For instance, in some cultures, openly expressing anger may be deemed unacceptable, leading individuals to suppress or redirect their anger, while in others, anger may be readily expressed and accepted.

Environmental factors such as stress, socioeconomic conditions, or access to resources can also contribute to anger and disappointment. Living in chronic stress or experiencing adverse circumstances can increase the likelihood of experiencing these emotions. Additionally, socioeconomic factors like poverty or inequality may create environments where individuals are more likely to experience anger and disappointment due to unmet needs or unfair treatment.

By exploring all these factors, we can gain a deeper understanding of the complex nature of anger and disappointment. This knowledge allows us to develop strategies and interventions that address the root causes and help individuals better manage and cope with these emotions.

Anger and disappointment are complex emotions that often mask deeper underlying feelings. When we experience anger, it is often a response to a perceived threat or a loss of control. Similarly, disappointment arises when our expectations are unmet, causing feelings of sadness and frustration. However, if we take the time to explore these emotions further, we can uncover a multitude of underlying emotions such as fear, sadness, and frustration.

Peeling back the layers of anger and disappointment allows us to gain a more comprehensive understanding of ourselves and our reactions. By uncovering these deeper emotions, we can explore the root causes of our anger and disappointment, which might be related to past experiences, insecurities, or unresolved issues. Understanding the underlying emotions helps us approach our feelings with more self-awareness and empathy.

For instance, beneath anger, we might find fear - fear of being hurt, fear of rejection, or fear of failure. By recognizing this fear, we can address it directly and work towards overcoming it, rather than simply reacting with anger. Similarly, disappointment may reveal underlying feelings of sadness and frustration, which can be explored to understand our expectations, desires, and needs more deeply.

By examining these layers of emotions, we can develop a more nuanced perspective. Instead of merely reacting impulsively to anger or disappointment, we can pause, reflect, and identify the core issues that triggered these emotions. This introspection allows us to gain insights into our triggers, patterns of behavior, and unhealthy coping mechanisms.

Moreover, this process enables us to respond to our emotions with greater self-awareness and compassion. Instead of directing anger outwardly or wallowing in disappointment, we can acknowledge our emotions and act from a place of empathy towards ourselves and others. We can develop healthier strategies for managing our emotions, such as utilizing positive self-talk, seeking support from loved ones, or engaging in activities that promote well-being.

Ultimately, unraveling the layers of anger and disappointment leads us towards personal growth and emotional healing. It allows us to better navigate our relationships, communicate effectively, and find resolutions to conflicts.

Section 2: The Destructive Power of Anger and Disappointment

When relationships are in turmoil, uncontrolled anger and disappointment can be major contributors to the chaos. These powerful emotions have the potential to wreak havoc by alienating our loved ones, friends, and colleagues. They can erode trust, breed resentment, and ultimately damage the very connections that are essential for healthy relationships.

Uncontrolled anger is often expressed through hurtful words, aggressive behavior, or even physical violence. When we fail to regulate our anger, it can escalate conflicts, making conversations unproductive and emotionally charged. This destructive expression of anger not only inflicts pain on those we care about but also creates a sense of fear and insecurity, driving a wedge between individuals.

Similarly, disappointment can be equally harmful to relationships. Persistent disappointment can lead to feelings of resentment, as unmet expectations may cause one party to start doubting the efforts or intentions of the other. Moreover, disappointment can bring about a sense of betrayal or letdown, making it difficult for individuals to trust each other and continue fostering a healthy connection.

As these negative emotions take center stage in relationships, the importance of self-reflection becomes apparent. It becomes necessary to question why anger and disappointment have become the prevailing emotions and to explore their underlying causes. This exploration can prompt individuals to evaluate their own behaviors, beliefs, and communication patterns, allowing for personal growth and understanding.

Fostering healthy communication is crucial in overcoming relationship turmoil. It involves being aware of our emotions, learning to express them in a constructive manner, and actively listening to others without judgment. Healthy communication also requires empathy, as it enables individuals to understand the perspectives and experiences of those they are in a relationship with.

Emotional regulation is another key aspect of maintaining healthy relationships. It involves recognizing and managing one's emotions effectively, preventing them from spiraling out of control. This doesn't mean suppressing emotions but rather finding healthy outlets for their expression, such as engaging in calming activities or seeking support from a trusted friend or therapist.

By fostering healthy communication and practicing emotional regulation, individuals can work towards repairing relationships in turmoil. Rebuilding trust, managing conflicts, and cultivating empathy are essential steps toward healing damaged connections. It is through these efforts that relationships have the potential to grow stronger and become more resilient in the face of future challenges.

When we are under the influence of anger and disappointment, our ability to make reasoned and rational decisions can become compromised. These emotions have a powerful impact on our thought processes, clouding our judgment and distorting our perception of the situation at hand.

Anger, for instance, often leads to impulsive and reactive behavior. When we are consumed by anger, our ability to think logically and consider different perspectives diminishes. We may become fixated on our own feelings of resentment and seek immediate retaliation or vindication, disregarding the potential consequences of our actions.

Disappointment, on the other hand, can lead to a sense of disillusionment and discouragement, which can impact our motivation and willingness to make wise decisions. In a state of disappointment, our outlook may be colored by negative biases, causing us to focus on what has gone wrong rather than objectively evaluating the options available to us.

Both anger and disappointment can impair our objectivity. They can cloud our ability to accurately assess the situation, leading us to make decisions based on emotional impulses rather than thoughtful analysis. This can leave us more susceptible to making choices that we may later regret and further fuel our feelings of disappointment.

However, by recognizing the influence of these emotions on our decision-making processes, we can strive for clarity and rationality. Taking a step back and allowing ourselves some time to calm down before making important decisions can help us regain perspective and approach the situation more objectively.

It is also important to actively challenge our biases and assumptions. By questioning our initial reactions and considering alternative viewpoints, we can identify potential flaws in our thinking and make more informed decisions.

Seeking support from others can be beneficial as well. Sharing our concerns and frustrations with trusted individuals can offer different perspectives and insights that we may have overlooked in the heat of the moment.

Furthermore, engaging in practices that promote emotional well-being, such as mindfulness or exercise, can help build resilience and emotional balance, reducing the likelihood of negative emotions influencing our decision-making.

In summary, anger and disappointment can significantly impair our decision-making abilities by clouding our judgment and leading us to act impulsively. However, by acknowledging the impact of these emotions, striving for objectivity, seeking support, and promoting emotional well-being, we can make more reasoned and thoughtful decisions, avoiding potential regrets and disappointments.

Section 3: Constructively Harnessing Anger and Disappointment

Embracing mindfulness involves incorporating therapeutic interventions into our lives, such as mindfulness practices, to help manage and channel emotions like anger and disappointment in a constructive manner. Mindfulness is the practice of intentionally focusing our attention on the present moment without judgment.

When we experience anger or disappointment, our initial response may be to react impulsively. This can lead to detrimental outcomes and poor decision-making. However, by cultivating present-moment awareness through mindfulness, we can create space within ourselves to acknowledge and validate these emotions.

Instead of suppressing or denying our anger and disappointment, mindfulness allows us to bring a non-judgmental and compassionate attitude towards these emotions. We learn to observe these emotions without becoming overwhelmed by them. By acknowledging and accepting these emotions, we create a safe and supportive inner environment.

With this foundation of mindfulness, we can then choose deliberate responses to these emotions rather than reacting impulsively. We are able to take a step back, reflect on the situation, and consider our options. This space helps us respond in a way that aligns with our values and goals, rather than reacting in ways that may be regretted later.

Mindfulness also helps us develop emotional resilience. By observing our anger and disappointment without judgment, we learn to tolerate and manage these emotions more effectively. We become better equipped to navigate challenging situations with greater composure and clarity.

Additionally, mindfulness cultivates a sense of self-awareness. We become attuned to the triggers that elicit anger and disappointment within us, allowing us to respond proactively rather than reactively. By understanding the patterns and underlying causes of these emotions, we can address them at their root instead of just addressing the surface-level manifestations.

In summary, embracing mindfulness means integrating therapeutic interventions, particularly mindfulness practices, into our lives to manage and channel anger and disappointment constructively. Through cultivating present-moment awareness, we create the space to acknowledge and validate these emotions while choosing deliberate responses instead of reacting impulsively. This practice ultimately leads to greater emotional resilience, self-awareness, and wiser decision-making.

Anger and disappointment are often seen as negative emotions that we instinctively try to avoid or suppress. However, when we are willing to delve into these emotions and truly understand their root causes, we can unlock tremendous potential for inner growth.

When we experience anger or disappointment, it is typically in response to a situation or event that hasn't aligned with our expectations or desires. It can feel overwhelming and frustrating, but instead of letting these feelings consume us, we can view them as valuable opportunities for self-reflection.

By actively embracing and exploring our anger and disappointment, we open ourselves up to understanding the deeper reasons behind our emotional responses. This requires a willingness to honestly examine our values, beliefs, and expectations and question whether they are serving us or holding us back.

For example, if we find ourselves consistently getting angry when things don't go our way, it may be a sign that we have unrealistic expectations or a need for control. By acknowledging this, we can adjust our perspective and learn to let go of attachments to outcomes, developing a sense of resilience and adaptability.

Similarly, disappointment can help us evaluate whether we are placing too much importance on external validation or relying too heavily on certain outcomes for our happiness. It can prompt us to reevaluate our priorities and shift our focus towards inner fulfillment instead of relying on external factors.

Working through these emotions can be challenging and uncomfortable, but the growth that comes from this process is worth the effort. By facing and understanding our anger and disappointment, we can gain new insights about ourselves, our relationships, and the world around us.

This inner growth allows us to become more self-aware, empathetic, and compassionate individuals. It helps us develop the strength to navigate adversity and find meaning in our experiences, even the ones that initially caused us anger or disappointment. Through this process, we discover new qualities within ourselves and uncover the capacity for growth and transformation.

In summary, embracing emotions such as anger and disappointment can be transformative. By using them as catalysts for self-reflection, we are better able to understand our values, beliefs, and expectations. Through this process, we develop resilience, gain new insights, and find deeper meaning in our experiences, ultimately fostering inner growth and transformation.

Section 4: Finding Meaning in the Wake of Anger and Disappointment

Cultivating forgiveness is a powerful and transformative process that involves seeking forgiveness, both for ourselves and others. It is essential for healing from anger, disappointment, and other negative emotions that can hinder our emotional well-being.

Forgiveness is significant in finding closure. When we hold onto anger and resentment, we are unable to move forward and find resolution in our lives. By seeking forgiveness, we acknowledge our own mistakes and take responsibility for our actions. This self-reflection allows us to let go of negative emotions and begin the healing process.

Forgiveness also fosters compassion. When we forgive others, we put ourselves in their shoes and try to understand their perspectives. This understanding leads to empathy and compassion, which can strengthen our relationships with others and promote a sense of connectedness and harmony. Cultivating forgiveness not only benefits our own emotional well-being but also positively impacts the people around us.

Moreover, forgiveness plays a crucial role in promoting emotional well-being. Holding onto anger, resentment, and grudges can have detrimental effects on our mental health. It can lead to increased stress, anxiety, and even depression. By consciously choosing forgiveness, we free ourselves from the burden of negative emotions, creating space for peace, happiness, and emotional stability in our lives.

Letting go of resentment through forgiveness also paves the way for personal growth. When we forgive, we release the toxic energy that holds us back from reaching our full potential. Forgiveness allows us to focus on personal development, learn from our past experiences, and strive for self-improvement. It provides an opportunity for self-reflection, leading to a deeper understanding of ourselves and our values.

In addition, forgiveness is instrumental in rebuilding relationships. When conflicts arise, forgiveness is the key to repairing and restoring trust. It allows us to rebuild bridges and move towards a healthier and more fulfilling connection with others. By forgiving, we create an environment of understanding, respect, and open communication, allowing relationships to thrive and grow stronger.

In conclusion, cultivating forgiveness is a vital step in healing from anger and disappointment. By seeking forgiveness, we find closure and let go of negative emotions. It fosters compassion, promotes emotional well-being, and supports personal growth. By forgiving others and ourselves, we create the space for acceptance, personal development, and the rebuilding of relationships. It is a transformative process that leads to greater peace, happiness, and emotional well-being.

In our day-to-day lives, we often find ourselves facing situations that trigger anger or disappointment. It could be a failed project at work, a relationship falling apart, or an unmet expectation. However, what truly matters is how we navigate through these emotions and come out stronger on the other side.

One key aspect of this process is redefining our expectations. Many times, our anger or disappointment stems from having set unrealistic goals for ourselves or others. By revisiting these expectations and aligning them with reality, we can prevent ourselves from falling into a cycle of negativity and frustration.

Setting realistic goals involves considering various factors such as our capabilities, resources, and external circumstances. It requires us to have a clear understanding of what is genuinely achievable within a given time frame. Taking into account these factors helps us set achievable, measurable, and time-bound goals that are more likely to be accomplished. By doing so, we pave the way for positive outcomes and reduce the chances of disappointment.

Practicing gratitude is another essential strategy that helps us navigate anger and disappointment. When we focus on gratitude, we train our minds to appreciate the positive aspects of our life rather than solely focusing on what went wrong. It helps us shift our perspective and find solace in the things that are going well. This doesn't mean ignoring problems or suppressing negative emotions, but rather acknowledging both the challenges and the blessings we have. Cultivating gratitude allows us to build emotional resilience and helps us cope with setbacks more effectively.

Embracing flexibility is equally important when dealing with anger and disappointment. Life is unpredictable, and it rarely goes according to plan. By developing the ability to adapt and be flexible, we can approach challenges with an open mind and willingness to change our approach if needed. Being rigid in our expectations, on the other hand, can lead to increased frustration and resistance when things don't go as planned. By embracing flexibility, we give ourselves the freedom to explore alternative paths and find new opportunities amidst the challenges.

Through the process of redefining expectations, practicing gratitude, and embracing flexibility, we cultivate resilience.

Resilience allows us to bounce back from setbacks, learn from our experiences, and find contentment even in the face of adversity. It doesn't mean that we never experience anger or disappointment, but rather, it equips us with the tools to navigate through these emotions in a healthier and more constructive way.

In conclusion, redefining expectations, practicing gratitude, and embracing flexibility are practical strategies that help us navigate anger and disappointment. By setting realistic goals, appreciating what we have, and adapting to change, we cultivate resilience and find contentment amidst life's inevitable challenges. Ultimately, these strategies empower us to overcome obstacles and embrace a more positive and fulfilling life.

In this chapter, we have ventured into the tumultuous torrents of anger and disappointment, seeking to understand their origins, consequences, and transformational potential. By unraveling their underlying causes, we can begin to navigate these emotions with greater self-awareness and empathy. Through mindfulness, personal growth, and the reevaluation of expectations, we can harness the potent energy of anger and disappointment constructively, finding meaning in their turbulent wake. Remember, within the storm lies the opportunity for growth and renewal, guiding us towards a deeper understanding of ourselves and others.

Chapter 6: Fear and it's transformative power

As humans, fear is ingrained in our very beings. It is a primal instinct that has been passed down through generations, an evolutionary mechanism designed to keep us safe and alive. When faced with danger, fear triggers a cascade of physiological responses within our bodies, preparing us for fight or flight.

But fear extends beyond mere survival instincts. It seeps into every aspect of our lives, manifesting in different forms and influencing our decisions. We fear failure, rejection, and judgment. We fear the unknown and the uncertain. We fear losing loved ones and being alone. Fear, it seems, is an ever-present companion on our journey through life.

In order to understand the transformative power of fear, we must first acknowledge its presence and uncover its roots. It is when we shine a light on our fears that we strip them of their power, enabling us to take control. For fear, although often seen as a hindrance, can actually be a catalyst for growth and change.

Take, for example, the fear of failure. Many of us are familiar with the sinking feeling in our stomachs when faced with the possibility of not meeting our own or others' expectations. We avoid taking risks, settling for mediocrity and stifling our potential. However, when we confront this fear head-on, we realize that failure is not the end, but rather a stepping stone towards success. It forces us to learn from our mistakes, adapt, and try again. Failure, when embraced, can transform our lives, propelling us towards greatness.

Similarly, the fear of rejection is a powerful force that often holds us back from pursuing our dreams and forming meaningful connections. We build walls around ourselves, afraid of being vulnerable and facing the pain of rejection. Yet, it is through vulnerability that we truly connect with others and experience the depth of human emotions. By embracing the fear of rejection, we open ourselves up to the possibility of profound connections and experiences that can shape our lives for the better.

Collectively, fear plays a significant role in shaping our societal narratives. It can fuel prejudice, discrimination, and hatred. It can divide communities and breed animosity. However, fear can also unite us and be a catalyst for change. Throughout history, it has been fear of injustice and inequality that has mobilized social movements and sparked revolutions. By harnessing this collective fear and channeling it towards positive change, we can transform society and create a better future for all.

In order to harness the transformative power of fear, we must confront it with courage and self-awareness. We must challenge the limiting beliefs and narratives that fear instills within us. We must not allow fear to dictate our choices, but rather use it as a guide to navigate the challenges that life presents.

It is through this transformative journey, embracing fear and the lessons it teaches, that we uncover our true potential. It is by facing our fears that we grow, evolve, and become the best versions of ourselves. Fear, once seen as our greatest adversary, becomes our ally in personal development and self-discovery.

As we embark on the path of transformation, let us remember that fear is not the enemy, but rather a powerful tool for growth. Let us embrace fear and harness its transformative power, allowing it to shape and guide us towards a life filled with purpose, resilience, and fulfillment.

Chapter 7: Love the elixir of life

Love, the elixir of life, is a force that permeates every aspect of our existence. It is the thread that weaves together the tapestry of human connection, giving us meaning and purpose in a vast and often uncertain world. As we delve into this complex emotion, we are confronted with the intricacies of its many forms and the profound impact it has on our lives.

Romantic love, with its heady blend of passion and desire, is a force that can ignite our souls and set our hearts ablaze. It is a force that can consume us completely, turning even the most logical minds into a cloud of fervent emotions. Adrift in the turbulent sea of romance, we find ourselves lost and yet found, vulnerable and yet empowered. It is here that we truly begin to understand the power of love, for it is in the realm of romance that we experience the heights of joy and the depths of despair.

But love is not confined to the realm of romance alone. It extends far beyond the boundaries of physical attraction and delves into the depths of familial bonds. The love between parent and child, sibling and sibling, is a foundation upon which we build our sense of belonging and security. It is a love that transcends time and space, connecting us to our roots and grounding us in a world that is ever-changing. In the embrace of familial love, we find solace and strength, knowing that we are never truly alone.

And then, there is the transformative power of unconditional love. It is a love that knows no bounds, that transcends flaws and imperfections, and that endures through the trials and tribulations of life. It is a love that inspires us to be better, to rise above our own limitations, and to embrace the beauty of our shared humanity. This love, although often elusive and rare, holds the potential to heal wounds and mend broken hearts.

As we navigate the labyrinthine pathways of love, we are confronted with many questions. What is the essence of love?

How does it shape us? Is it a product of our own desires, or does it exist beyond the realm of our understanding? Through a blend of poignant stories, philosophical musings, and psychological insights, we endeavor to capture the true significance of love in our lives.

In our exploration, we uncover the delicate balance between vulnerability and strength that love demands of us. We discover that love requires us to open our hearts and expose ourselves to the possibility of pain, for it is through this vulnerability that we find true connection. Love is not without risk, but it is through taking these risks that we discover our own capacity for growth and transformation.

Ultimately, love is the elixir of life, for it sustains and nourishes our souls. It is an emotion that defies classification or quantification, for its power lies in its ability to transcend words and boundaries. It is an emotion that can lift us to the heights of ecstasy and plunge us into the depths of despair. Yet, it is in this dichotomy that we find the true beauty of love, for it is through experiencing its many facets that we come to understand the full range of human emotion.

Chapter 7 is a tribute to love, a reflection on its many dimensions, and an exploration of its profound impact on our lives. It is a chapter that seeks to demystify the enigma of love and shed light on its true significance. As we delve into its depths, we are reminded of the power of love to shape our deepest connections and inspire our most profound transformations. Love, the elixir of life, is a force that can heal wounds, ignite passions, and bind us together in a world that often feels fragmented.

To love

In the realm of heart's sweetest desire,
Where love's wings unfurl and souls take flight,
A symphony of emotions set afire,
An ode to love, both day and night.

Love, an enchantress with gentle touch,
Whispers in winds, a melodious refrain,
A tapestry woven from love's golden clutch,
Binding hearts, like a celestial chain.

When love blossoms, seraphic and pure,
It paints our world in vibrant hue,
A tender touch, a passionate lure,
Unveiling secrets that once were few.

Love transcends barriers, bridges divide,
Beyond borders, cultures, and creed,
A language universal, love shall confide,
A path paved with compassion's lead.

Within love's embrace, we find solace,
Eclipsing sorrows, healing every scar,
Two souls entwined, a sacred promise,
Strength in unity, love's shining star.

Through love's prism, we see anew,
The true essence of hearts intertwined,
A kaleidoscope of feelings imbue,
An eternal flame, forever assigned.

So let us celebrate love's magic spell,
Embrace its wonders with hearts aglow,
For love, the tale we forever shall tell,
A testament to love's eternal flow.

From Love

Epilogue: The Emotional Odyssey Continues...

As we come to the end of this exploration into the realm of emotions, it becomes clear that our emotional journeys are not static. They are constantly changing and evolving, influenced by the experiences we encounter, the relationships we form, and the passage of time. Just as life itself is a journey, so too are our emotions.

Throughout this odyssey, we have only scratched the surface of the vast depth and breadth of human emotions. There are countless pathways still left unexplored, hidden beneath the surface of our consciousness. The vast array of emotions we are capable of experiencing is both mysterious and fascinating, and our understanding of them is never complete.

This book serves as a guide, providing insight and understanding into the enigmatic nature of our feelings. It invites us to continue delving into the depths of our emotions, to seek a deeper understanding of ourselves and those around us. It encourages us to embrace the dynamic nature of our emotional landscape, to stay curious and open-minded as we navigate the ever-changing terrain of our own hearts.

For it is in the journeys of our hearts that we find the true beauty of life. It is not solely in the destination, but in the experiences, connections, and growth that occur along the way. Our emotions are not meant to be stagnant or fixed, but fluid and transformative. They shape us, mold us, and offer us opportunities for self-discovery and personal growth.

By continually exploring our emotions, we learn more about ourselves, our desires, our fears, and our dreams. We develop a more profound understanding of the human experience and cultivate empathy for the emotions of others. Through this understanding, we can forge deeper connections with the people around us, fostering compassion, love, and mutual support.

In this ongoing journey, we discover that our emotions are not something to be feared or suppressed but embraced and cherished. They are the vibrant hues that color the canvas of our lives, adding depth, richness, and meaning. By acknowledging the full spectrum of our emotions, both light and dark, we can truly embrace the complexity of being human.

So, as we conclude this odyssey through the realm of emotions, let us remember that our emotional journeys are never complete. There will always be more to explore, more to learn, and more to feel. May this book serve as a catalyst for personal growth, self-reflection, and a greater appreciation of the complexities of our emotional lives. And may we continue to embark on the beautiful, ever-evolving journeys of our hearts.

1. "Love is composed of a single soul inhabiting two bodies." - Aristotle
2. "The greatest happiness of life is the conviction that we are loved; loved for ourselves, or rather, loved in spite of ourselves." - Victor Hugo
3. "Love is not about how much you say 'I love you,' but how much you prove that it's true." - Unknown

Author's note:

Dear readers,

I want to express my heartfelt gratitude for taking the time to embark on this emotional journey with me. Writing this book has been a labor of love, and it brings me joy to know that it has resonated with you. The exploration of emotions, particularly love, is an ongoing odyssey that shapes our existence. I hope that this book has served as a guide, shedding light on the intricacies and deepening our comprehension of this enigmatic force.

Thank you for allowing me to be a part of your own personal voyage of understanding. May this book inspire you to continually explore the depths of your own emotions and foster a greater appreciation for the journeys of the heart.

With heartfelt appreciation,

Jason Alexander

ABOUT THE AUTHOR

Jason Alexander

Jason is a passionate father, husband, and is diagnosed with ADHD. He seeks to change the narrative from disorder to Gifted. Starting with himself, one book at a time.

Made in the USA
Middletown, DE
07 April 2024

52621727R00022